A Nurse Leader's

LITTLE

Instruction Book

The Ultimate Resource for Retaining Staff

JEANNA BOZELL, RN, CPC

A Nurse Leader's Little Instruction Book: The Ultimate Resource for Retaining Staff

ISBN 0-9729603-0-9
Copyright © 2003 by Jeanna Bozell
1st Printing

Published by NurseQuest®
A division of Professional Resource Group, Inc.
Muncie, Indiana

Cover design by: Arrick Garringer of CS Kern, Inc.

Printed in the United States of America.

Acknowledgments

I sincerely wish to thank our peer reviewers for their time and expertise: Doreen C. Johnson, RN, MA, CHE; Kathy A. Howell, RN, BSN, MA, SPHR; Jerry M. Bozell, SPHR.

My appreciation to Steve Helm, Jan Goff, John C. Maxwell, Stephen R. Covey, Rick Warren, John Townsend, and Henry Cloud for their time, energies, and/or resources, through which I have been mentored.

I'd also like to recognize these insightful leaders for their timeless quotes used in this book: Indira Gandhi, Napoleon Bonaparte, Ralph Waldo Emerson, Johann von Goethe, Homer, Winston Churchill, Thomas Fuller, Oliver Wendell Holmes, Henry Ward Beecher, Native American saying, Voltaire, Henry D. Thoreau, Edmund Burke, Benjamin Disraeli, Benjamin Franklin, Friedrich Nietzsche, Lao-tzu, Robert Louis Stevenson, Thomas Carlyle, Mark Twain, and Abraham Lincoln.

Introduction

The nursing shortage continues to impact hospitals nationwide as healthcare employers do everything in their power to fill positions. Offering sign-on bonuses and perks is a quick fix but only a short-term solution. The reality is that if nurses aren't happy, they won't stay. Here's what I've learned during my 13+ years as a nurse consultant: recruitment is sales—retention is leadership. Through conversations with literally thousands of nurses in the job market, I've discovered the top reasons nurses leave their jobs. More than half of those reasons had to do with their direct supervisor. Money was near the bottom of the list! I created this book so that you, too, can understand what needs to be done and why. It's probably not what you *want* to hear, but it is what you *need* to hear . . . if you want to keep quality staff.

It will cost you something . . . a change in behavior, getting out of your comfort zone, and redirecting some of your time and resources. But if you commit to these practices and principles, your new actions will ignite change in your staff. I have faith in you, faith in your desire to grow, and faith in your leadership!

Remember, the leadership journey is best when walked together!

Your friend,

Jeanna

NOTHING is more powerful or more fragile than the human spirit. The opportunity to influence that spirit is one of the most incredible privileges of being a leader.

The relationship a person has with her supervisor is the single-
most important relationship in her work life.
If that relationship is good, she feels valued, positive,
and able to handle challenges. If it is bad, she feels misunderstood,
angry, unappreciated, and tense. If you were a patient, which nurse
would you want to answer your call light?
Choose to create a positive environment on your unit.

I suppose leadership at one time meant muscles;
but today it means getting along with people.

—*Indira Gandhi*

Fear is the driving force behind negativity . . . fear of the unknown,
fear of losing something, fear of discomfort, fear of the loss of
(perceived) control, fear of change, etc. Face your fears . . . focus
on your mission, obtain knowledge, and take action!

Try to remember that an employee is doing the best he can with
what he has at any given point in time. For better results, enhance
the tools he has to work with through mentoring, teaching,
encouraging growth, and holding him accountable.

A leader guides her team through many challenges . . . serving as a light of hope and direction so team members can find their way, even on the most treacherous of paths. Don't let your light go out. Recharge your battery often!

A common generational need that is important to every staff member is quality of work life.

If it is important to your staff, then it *must* be important to you.

Use a third party company to ask exit interview questions to all *current* employees, not just *exiting* employees. By using an outside firm, employees can be truthful and not pay a consequence. Getting a jump on the issues saves the high cost of filling openings later and also helps build a solid team. But don't wait for your organization to act. It's ultimately your responsibility to continually listen, ask questions, and know your team on a daily basis.

FEAR is a contagious condition
. . . especially when the leader
is the carrier!

Buy leadership books, audio tapes, and CDs. Put them everywhere you spend time . . . the office, bedroom, bathroom, garage, kitchen, and in the car. Think of the education you will get while waiting for a train, driving to work, waiting for your children or spouse, taking a shower, cooking dinner, changing the oil, cleaning house, etc. Make time to grow. Never become ordinary!

Create a learning environment for your staff and involve them in teaching each other. Each week, have a staff member bring in something to teach her peers—to enhance professional growth with either a clinical or leadership-based topic. The team can show appreciation with a small reward for her efforts!

Read *The 21 Irrefutable Laws of Leadership* by John C. Maxwell.

Nothing is more difficult, and therefore more precious, than to be able to decide.

—*Napoleon Bonaparte*

Forgive and move forward. Forgiveness does not mean that what the person did was okay; it only means that the person no longer owes you anything for what she did. A harbored grudge makes for an unfair judge . . . *and for dysfunctional communication.* Work hard to keep relationships in good repair!

Be accessible to your staff. Give them your attention, show them they are a priority, and communicate this by what you say and what you do.

Encourage a team member to become certified in his area of clinical specialty. Make sure to follow your own advice!

Trust men and they will be true to you; treat them greatly and they will show themselves great.

—*Ralph Waldo Emerson*

Expecting a successful outcome goes a long way
in determining a victory.

Develop a hunger for learning. If you wanted to be a pilot, you'd
take lessons and become certified. The same goes for being a
leader. If you're going to lead, make sure you give yourself the
absolute best chance to be effective and go at it with 100% of your
effort. If not, you're setting yourself up to fail.

An unsure or pessimistic leader transmits
a lack of confidence to his staff.

Prioritize effective communication. Assumptions are deadly
. . . to your leadership.

Ask a team member, "How can I make your job easier?"
Removing barriers to getting the job done elevates staff morale
and improves customer satisfaction!

When a person's reaction to a situation is out of proportion to
what the situation warrants, it usually means there is another
underlying issue. Ask questions.

Change the way you think. There have never been so many openings for nurses and so few nurses to fill them . . . and it will only get worse. Don't say, "They're fortunate to work here," but say instead, "We're fortunate to have them."

Are you having trouble making a decision involving staff or your unit? Reread your organization's mission statement. Make sure the decision you reach is in alignment with the purpose of your organization.

We must always change, renew, rejuvenate ourselves; otherwise we harden.

—*Johann von Goethe*

ACQUIRE THE FIRE! In fact, create it! The fire of enthusiasm must be fed with action, vision, continuous resources, and new ideas. Don't wait around for spontaneous combustion.

The quick fix to the staffing crisis is bribery to get nurses in the door. However, the long term answer to keeping valuable employees is leadership. It's a fact, it's that simple, and it won't change. What one thing, if you did it everyday, would help you better connect with your staff?

Take quiet time alone to allow your dreams and ideas time to develop. If you stay busy, you will either miss the opportunity or you won't take the time to act on it when you have a dream.

Mark your calendar so that every other month, you will read at least one self-development or leadership book, such as Steven R. Covey's *The 7 Habits of Highly Effective People.*

The greatest challenge of a leader isn't staff development, it is self-development.

THE GROUNDS FOR LEADERSHIP

MIDDLE GROUND is not where it's at! Be bold. Make decisions.

COMMON GROUND is crucial for connecting
with your staff! Find it!

HIGHER GROUND must be strived for at all times. Grow there!

SOLID GROUND is your foundation, your values
based on principles . . . doing what's right.

A micromanager's focus is small. Her actions may stem from selfishness, control, fear of failure, poor self image, or no confidence in her team. The mission of the organization or the good of her staff isn't considered. Everything is viewed by way of, "How will this affect me?" She tells people what to do, how to do it, and then shows up to supervise or does it herself. She doesn't trust her staff; her staff doesn't trust her. There are no happy people in this picture. Everyone loses—the leader, the staff, the patients, and the organization. Empower your people!

Address poor performance issues immediately. Initially, the staff will resent the employee for not doing her job. After a while, they will resent you for not doing yours.

The creation of a thousand forests is in one acorn.

—*Ralph Waldo Emerson*

Keep confidential things confidential.

If you are a Chief Nursing Officer or Director and have no contact with your staff nurses, you have a lot of work to do! Step out of your office just a few minutes each day. As you walk through the halls, smile and say, "Good morning." Positive comments work wonders: "I see that you hit the ground running this morning." You can't build meaningful relationships with 50 people. But you can show, by taking time to learn names, saying "Hello," and commenting on something positive, that you appreciate them. They need to know you are real. If you are too busy to invest a few minutes a day, you are too busy!

The fact is . . . you can't do what you do without them!

Staff members will disappoint you. They are human.
Care about them anyway.

To motivate your team, give them something to work towards
and commit to—a purpose.

Real leaders know, "It's not about me."

Five people working together for a common purpose
have an exponentially greater effect than the sum of five people
working alone. Value teamwork, reward it, and put it high
on your list of priorities!

Believe in yourself . . . it's absolutely necessary in order for your
staff to believe in you.

FOR REAL LEADERS ONLY: As a group, ask your staff to do an
evaluation of you as their leader. You may be surprised by what you
learn. It could be the most important appraisal you ever get!

Give a gift subscription to a professional journal, such as *Nursing Management*®, as a reward or recognition for going above and beyond the call of duty.

Keep your promises.

Ask a team member, "What are you passionate about?" Enjoy hearing their enthusiasm. Don't miss out on the gifts and energies of your team!

Lead with a HIRE PURPOSE: Hire people who share the team's values. A major source of stress for supervisors and employees is having different values and trying to work together. It's frustrating for both parties involved. If values aren't shared, misery will follow. It's not that one is right and one is wrong. It simply isn't a good fit for either party.

Change the way you look at things. Imagine for a moment that most of your team called in sick today. The next staff person you see is the only one who showed up for work. Will the greeting you give her make her feel valued? Never take your staff for granted.

Think. Think often. *How can you make a difference? What can you do to impact the people and situations around you?* Leading means doing; it means getting involved, making things happen. Being passive is not an option for effective leadership.

The hearts of great men can be changed.

—*Homer*

LEADERSHIP is not self-service,
it's full-service.

When conflict arises, having compassion for an employee and the situation she is in communicates that you respect and value her. It is always easier to take constructive criticism from someone who cares about you than from someone who doesn't. First, listen compassionately and always take the opportunity to understand what she is relating to you. Remember, *how* you say it is just as important as *what* you say.

Teach and inspire. You will reap *what* you sow and you will reap *more* than you sow. Compound your investment!

Be constantly on the lookout for raw talent . . . the diamond in the rough. It's our future!

Be proactive. Have a plan and be prepared. As preparation time increases, crisis intervention time decreases.

When the eagles are silent, the parrots begin to jabber.

—Winston Churchill

When evaluating staff, step into your teacher role. Be truthful, caring, and don't forget to begin and end with positives.

The employee who is the most resistant to your influence is the one who needs it the most. Don't give up on her!

Learn continuously. You cannot teach what you do not know.

Encourage team members.

Act only in the best interests of your team.

Dedicate yourself to effective communication.

Educate your team.

Resolve to be a person of character, integrity, and competence.

Encourage and cover the cost for a staff member to attend a conference, bring back information, and share it with her peers. Lead a round of applause for her efforts and give her a card of appreciation signed by every member of the team!

If you learn how to hire right, communicate effectively, educate and train your staff, build relationships, work on your leadership, and help your team balance work and home life, one day soon you may have a list of people waiting to work for you!
Work towards that goal.

LEADERSHIP is all about
relationships. Take an inch;
give a mile.

Get your group together and create a praise award for someone in a different department . . . lab, housekeeping, other clinical areas, cafeteria, maintenance, pharmacy, etc. Or *think way outside the box* and find a positive about someone on another shift!!! Build great relationships! If your team members are focused on finding positives in others, they will!

Be little. Don't belittle.

Did you ever have one of those days? A day when everything seemed to go wrong? You know what it's like to feel helpless, hopeless, and overwhelmed. Be on the lookout for that person and give an encouraging word. Your kindness won't soon be forgotten.

Buy books of $1 gift certificates from fast food restaurants and use those individually for small tokens of appreciation. They add up! Who says there's no free lunch?

It's important to know: (1) if you do what you've always done, you'll get the same results, (2) when you change a behavior in yourself, your staff will respond differently to the new behavior, and (3) the results could be immediate AND amazing!

Today is yesterday's pupil.

—*Thomas Fuller*

Leave personal problems at home. That's why they are called "personal" problems.

Never underestimate the power of a word of encouragement
to a struggling team member.

Subscribe to or give a subscription to *NurseQuest Insights*®, a free
e-mail newsletter dedicated to the mentorship of nurse leaders.

Dysfunctional communication derails relationships . . . in
marriages, with parents, children, siblings, friends and neighbors,
and at work. Infrequent, inaccurate or misunderstood messages,
the silent treatment, and emotional outbursts are detrimental to
team-building, productivity, and future communication.

Maintain a leadership journal. Doing so will keep you focused and help you remain on course. Record your thoughts, your dreams, your plans, what worked, and what didn't. In time, you can look back and be more objective in assessing yourself and your leadership style!

You are a V.I.P.—a very influential person. Choose to influence those you lead in a positive way by nurturing, teaching, guiding, modeling, and having your team's best interests in mind. Not doing these things is also influencing them . . . in a negative way.

Build a card file for employee information . . . birthdays, passions, dislikes, hobbies, how they want to be rewarded, etc. You simply can't remember everything.

Ask your team, "What do you like about working on this unit?" If they can't think of anything, you'd better get busy!

Real leaders effectively lead staff through change by educating them, involving them, continually and accurately communicating factual information, encouraging them to vent, and showing care.

Decide what type of work environment you want to create
for your staff, and then do everything you can to make
that vision a reality.

Never underestimate the power of a sincere compliment.

Be open to flexible scheduling and job sharing. If you can help
employees to better juggle family and work, you will retain more
staff. If you make them choose, you will lose.

Are you known for being a resource to new nurses? How about those who have been there awhile but have less experience than you? Do they feel they can come to you if needed? Try to remember those early years as an R.N. and what that was like. Do your part to create great memories for the newer, less experienced nurses and pour yourself into their continual development.

A moment's insight is sometimes worth a life's experience.

—*Oliver Wendell Holmes*

Understand what your purpose is and why it is important. What will it mean to get there? Think through it, write it down, and tell others. Think about it, learn about it, and dream about it.

Once you do that, you will: (1) come up with new ideas, (2) notice things all around you that align with it, (3) be drawn to and find others having the same purpose, and (4) reflect it in your goals and accomplishments.

Request your team members' work or home e-mail addresses.
You can easily send educational information, book titles,
interesting nursing websites, notes, e-cards, praise, etc.
It's all about connecting!

The facility's leadership team made up of your peers can be a
tremendous source of support. Meet regularly to educate and learn
from each other. Find internal benchmarks. Who has the lowest
turnover? What are they doing to motivate staff? How have they
promoted team-building? Keep the agenda positive and moving
forward. It's not meant to be a gripe session.

Perception is reality, so make sure that all communication is clear, thorough, direct, and often. If you do not tell them, they will not know. If they hear it from someone else, the odds of it being accurate are slim to none.

If you want your staff to complete a specific task or behavior, help them understand the benefit of the action to them and to their patients . . . to buy into it on their own. What would cause you to decide it was something you wanted to do? Now, provide that information to your team.

Don't forget to reward yourself when you meet a goal or accomplish a job. Have a little fun!

The mind is absolutely incredible. A thought develops deep within it, then turns into a belief and sparks an action—and that action leads to the results that you get. Do you see how what you listen to and what you read can impact who you are?

Schedule time for yourself . . . to rest, to learn, to think, to plan, and to reassess. You can't be effective if you're running on empty!

Did you ever work for a boss you didn't like? One who taught you what not to do by her everyday actions? Step back and assess yourself as a supervisor. What parts of your leadership will a staff member take with her as she moves into her first leadership position? What parts will she want to leave behind?

Never underestimate the power of a smile.

Be humble.

A LEADER'S influence affects people's lives, both professionally and personally . . . and where that influence ends, no one can say.

Lead with a HIRE PURPOSE: Always verify an applicant's education and licensure. There may be times when you find a misrepresentation. It is better to learn up front than after a crisis.

A helping word to one in trouble is often like a switch on a railroad track . . . an inch between wreck and smooth, rolling prosperity.
—*Henry Ward Beecher*

Never underestimate the power of employee feedback.

Restore broken trust with commitment and diligence. Listen openly to the situation. Own up to your mistakes right then and there. Trying to talk your way out of it or around it will only compound your problem. Take responsibility for your actions. Apologize and ask for forgiveness. There may be a consequence to pay. If you can right the wrong, commit to do so. Find out what it will take to rebuild the trust. The process takes time, so be patient.

If you believe you can, you will. If you believe you can't, you won't. It's all on your shoulders . . . so to speak.

Be a Gossip-Buster! When you are in a conversation and gossip starts, say, "I think you need to talk directly to him about this."

Don't say negative things to one staff member about another staff member. This causes a lack of trust (a roadblock to further communication), hurt feelings . . . and breaks down the team.

Don't complain to your staff about your hours, your job, or your pay. Employees always think their boss has it better than they do and they will not understand your point of view.
The result is negative.

Preventing a crisis is much easier than dealing with one.

Tell me and I'll forget. Show me and I may not remember.
Involve me and I'll understand.

—*Native American saying*

Real leaders know that three things must take place to achieve effective communication: (1) listening, (2) speaking, and (3) understanding by both people involved.

If you can touch both the hearts and the minds of your employees, you will inspire . . . a mark of the most influential leader of all.

Don't put off difficult and dreaded tasks. They only get tougher.

Never forget . . . you and your team are on the same side!

You can't be a clock-watcher where relationships are concerned. People can tell when your mind is elsewhere. When that happens, they feel unimportant and disrespected. Invest in the moment!

Ask for input from your team. Ask questions. Challenge them to think! Don't ask for input if the decision is already made.

Avoid reacting to situations guided by emotions.
Staff members need to know what to expect
and what they can count on from you.

Say what you mean and mean what you say.

Ask a team member, "How would you know if you were
appreciated?" The answer may be different for each employee.
Record it and use the information wisely . . . it's invaluable!

IT'S EASY to be a victim without a plan of action.

Make a point to remember your employees' birthdays. What a perfect day to give a card, a candy bar, or a note to let them know they are important!

What one thing could your boss say to you that would make you feel valued? Say that to your staff. In fact, say that to your boss!

When counseling a team member, always ask, "If you had it to do over again, how would you handle it?"

Smile. Intentionally smile. You won't always feel like it, but if you do, you will feel even better! As the leader, your face reveals the state of the unit and your team is watching.

Don't beat yourself up. Reassess what happened, ask yourself what you would do differently, learn from it, and move on . . . a little wiser from the experience. Focusing on past issues keeps you, and those around you, from moving forward.

Take action. You can have a million brilliant ideas, but if you do not act on any one of them, nothing changes.

Getting to know and understand your organization's most valuable resource, your team, is the best investment you can make of your time.

Be crystal clear in communicating your expectations of staff . . . have them verbalize understanding.

Your attitude when resolving issues with a team member determines: (1) how seriously he will take what you say and (2) what he will do with that information. Decide on your goal before the meeting; make sure the results you seek are for his highest good. Explain your intentions up front. Look at these instances as an opportunity to teach, develop, and assist him to grow. Remember, the behaviors you address are probably the symptoms, not the cause. Look deeper; ask questions. Request his help to reach a solution.

Listen intently. It's one of the most important skills
you possess as a leader.

If you see a problem, don't think, "It's not my job to solve it."
Instead think, "What can I do to impact that problem,
to make a difference?"

Be an igniter. Make things happen!

Guilt is a negative motivator that breeds resentment and anger.

What is one way you can show a team member that you are interested in her work? Do it today!

Reassess regularly. If something isn't working, stop doing it. Do something different . . . ANYTHING. It's the only way you will get a different result!

Do you know the names of the housekeeping staff who work regularly on your unit(s)? Every person makes an impression on your patients and their families, they contribute to the overall atmosphere, and most important—they can benefit from your influence!

The moment someone tells a leader, "It's never been done before," is the very moment it becomes a challenge!

Be real. If you do not know something, admit it.

Your toughest leadership challenge can be your greatest mentoring tool. What you learn through the tough times is growth. Share your knowledge with another!

Be objective. Always try to put yourself in your staff's shoes . . . see things through their eyes. It's the best way to understand the other side, make fair decisions, and be compassionate.

Nagging occurs when consequences don't. Hold your team accountable for their actions and have good, consistent follow through.

Work every shift once in awhile. It gives you the opportunity to get to know staff members on other shifts, demonstrates that you care, and shows that you wouldn't ask them to do something you wouldn't do yourself. Let them know that they, too, are part of your team!

Find out what motivates each employee. It won't be the same for everyone . . . and just because it motivates you doesn't mean it will motivate him.

Initiate a voluntary book club for your leaders. For those who participate, choose a book and foot the bill. Ask them to read and make notes throughout their copy. Set a date approximately six weeks ahead to meet with them to discuss the contents and their thoughts. Supply refreshments. It's a great way to get several of your leaders on the same page (literally) and is more cost-effective than sending one person to a conference! The benefits are priceless.

Don't encourage competition among team members. It weakens
the unity and changes the focus to something
negative: "It's all about me."

We create fear in our minds by thinking of the bad things that could
happen. If it's something in your control, act on it. If not, replace
the negative focus with something positive.
Fear can be a paralyzing obsession.

Every job on your unit is important.

Is there anything so wise as to learn from the experience of others?

—*Voltaire*

Real leaders lead with their hearts. Adjust your focus from "What can this employee do for me?" to "How can I help her succeed?"

Never underestimate the power and destructiveness of gossip.

Lead with a HIRE PURPOSE: Make sure applicants understand the job. One reason nurses leave is because duties are misunderstood, misrepresented, or unclearly explained. Supply accurate information . . . not just a job description, but the real story. How many hours will she work? Is there an orientation program? Describe a typical day. Ask for her observations of the position. Then, at the end of the interview day ask, "Do you have *any* concerns about being able to do this job?" Effective communication is critical. Just because you know something doesn't mean she knows it. If she takes the job and it doesn't meet her expectations, she'll leave. And she will perceive it as misrepresentation, regardless of how it happened. Remember, perception is reality!

Work with your organization to provide resources to employees for professional growth: tuition reimbursement, time off and funds for obtaining certifications, conferences, subscriptions for professional journals, books, tapes, etc.

Never overestimate the accuracy of your communication. Accurate communication feels like over-communication. Do it anyway.

Your team has good ideas. Why not ask them?

Keep a "Quote of the Day" in a prominent place at the nurse's station. Every bit of positive input is a plus. Initiate a reward for the person who knows the quote when randomly approached. It will not only encourage them to read it, but to remember it. Invite team members to contribute quotes they find, too. Everyone will benefit!

Read *Principle-Centered Leadership* by Steven R. Covey.

You never know how or when your influence will change the very direction of a life.

Revamp your employee evaluation form to include the values of your team, not just job duties.
If you do, you will see those values modeled.

Before you enter into any conversation, make it your goal to understand. When an employee feels understood, the barriers are lowered and true communication takes place.

Make time for yourself.

Timing is everything. Addressing staff issues immediately means the difference between a mountain and a molehill. Early intervention prevents the escalation of negative behavior, hurt feelings, and a growing level of resentment. In fact, the earlier a negative behavior is handled, the less likely it is to be repeated. Attend to the spark before it becomes an inferno!

Your vision is the lens through which you see things . . . and that lens allows for conceiving new ways and new ideas to make a way for accomplishing your goals.
Vision is all about growth—and the future!

Ask a staff member, "If you could, what changes would you make on our unit(s)?

Everyone hears only what he understands.

—*Johann von Goethe*

TAKE AWAY the purpose . . .
and commitment evaporates
into thin air.

Put titles and roles aside. People are people. Do you treat everyone
. . . physicians, unit secretaries, patients, volunteers, staff
members, visitors, cafeteria staff, and employees from other units
as you would want to be treated . . . with respect,
patience, and courtesy?

Erect a team bulletin board where articles of interest can be posted
and shared. Make sure you participate, too!

You never know till you try to reach them how accessible men are;
but you must approach each man by the right door.

—*Henry Ward Beecher*

Communicate how your team's mission and goals tie into the organization's mission and goals. It helps them see how they contribute to the overall success and to feel like part of the organization as a whole.

Be patient with everyone, and especially with those who frustrate you.

Unforgiveness means a past hurt—and the pain of that hurt—recurs every time you think of it. Forgiveness releases you from that pain . . . and frees you to move forward and in a positive direction! Choose to forgive.

Every newly hired nurse should have an ample orientation followed up by being paired with a preceptor who is a positive and experienced role model.

Celebrate a positive result by buying a team shirt or cap, come up with a name for your team, and throw a party!

Work in tandem with the leadership team and create a Manager-Apprentice program. Partner a mentor with a "diamond-in-the-rough" to teach her the day-to-day operations of the unit and most important—what leadership is all about.

Lead with a HIRE PURPOSE: Never hire a person who has a negative attitude. Attitude affects everybody . . . patients, peers, subordinates, leadership, etc. A positive attitude rubs off on others; so does a negative one. Remember, a candidate who is interviewing is on her *best* behavior. Think what she'd be like as an employee!

Commit to CPQI: Continuous Personal Quality Improvement . . .
for your staff and for yourself.

We are always paid for our suspicion by finding what we expect.
—*Henry David Thoreau*

Watch for early signs of frustration in your staff. Show interest and
care. Verbalize what you see by saying, "You seem troubled." Then
simply listen. Sometimes being able to vent those frustrations is all
that is needed. Be a Conflict Prevention Specialist!

Victims are reactors. Don't be a victim of your circumstances, other people, your past, or heredity. Choose your response. It's at that very moment that you are empowered!

Rebuild a relationship that is in need of repair before day's end.

Which staff member can you depend on? Who is most responsible? Now commit your time and resources to mentoring her as a future leader. Remember, the leadership journey is best when walked together . . . but only a few will go with you.

Title doesn't mean leadership; your decision and commitment to lead does.

The best use of your time at work is to use it for something that will live on after you are gone . . . pour yourself into others.

No passion so effectively robs the mind of its powers of acting and reasoning as fear.

—*Edmund Burke*

If wages are fair, an employee will remain loyal as long as he feels that you care, value, and respect him.

If two people are the same, one is not necessary! Value the differences in your staff members.

Never lose your temper in front of your staff. Blowing up, even if it occurs rarely, leads to dysfunctional communication. Because staff members never know when something they say may hit you the wrong way, they will not be open and honest in *any* communication.

Sincerely compliment a staff member today, face to face.

The way you handle change directly affects how your team will handle it. Remain positive, keep them informed, involve them, communicate the vision, and encourage venting. Keep in mind that the entire organization is a team. It's not what happens to you, but what you do with what happens to you, that matters.

Find a mentor and learn as much as you can from that person. If *you* serve as your only role model, you greatly limit your growth potential.

Offer audio or video training at noon where staff can bring their lunch, eat, and learn at the same time. It generates the same result as coaching during a game's half-time. The positive atmosphere will inspire and your team will return revived, refocused, and back on track!

Constructive criticism presented in a caring way leads to positive change and growth.

The secret to success is constancy to purpose.

—*Benjamin Disraeli*

If a staff member asks to talk with you, do it within 24 hours . . . the sooner, the better. From an employee's viewpoint, the longer the wait, the less of a priority she is. Remember, what's important to her *must* be important to you.

Be proactive. Hope is great but the major ingredient in reaching a goal is action!

Be honest in all you say and do.

Focus on behavior that is in line with your principles and what you value: teamwork, quality patient care, positive attitude, going the extra mile, etc. and reward it as soon as possible. You will get more of the same in return!

The faultfinder will find faults even in paradise.

—*Henry David Thoreau*

Let your staff know you care about them. Then in everything you do, whether addressing a conflict or going through a major change, they will know your motives are pure.

Leading yourself is one of the most difficult tasks of a leader. Ask a trusted colleague to give honest insight into your leadership, strengths, and weaknesses. Then, objectively list how you see yourself. Compare the results and work not only to improve weaknesses, but also strengths.

See problems as challenges and opportunities for growth, not as obstacles.

Ask a team member, "Do you have a hobby?" The more you know about a person, the easier it is to connect . . . to talk about something of interest to him.

The more information you put into your brain, the more likely you are to come up with new ideas. Continue your journey of learning by attending at least one conference a year.

It's impossible for you to make an employee feel valuable if, deep down inside, you don't think that she is.

It takes a lot less time, effort, and money to talk with, listen to, and build strong relationships with your staff than it does to run ads, recruit, interview, and train their replacements.

Brag about your team to your supervisor and make sure that at least some of those team members are within earshot.

Make working on relationships a priority. Mark your calendar. Initiate at least one action every week toward that goal. As your relationships grow, you will see a definitive change in your effectiveness as a leader, the cohesiveness and morale of your team, and the results on your unit!

If you treat men the way they are, you never improve them. If you treat them the way you want them to be, you do.

—*Johann von Goethe*

Recruitment is sales. You can offer huge sign-on bonuses, large salaries, and perks to attract nurses to your facility. But keeping them is the challenge. Why? Retention is leadership. If you can help employees feel like they make a difference—that it matters that they are there—you will be ahead of most of your competition!

Are you a better leader than you were a year ago? What steps can you take to go to the next level?

Always counsel staff and handle conflict in private; praise anywhere and everywhere!

Do what you say you will do. You cannot lead effectively without integrity.

The hard lesson is this: If your staff doesn't respect you, then you will pay the consequences . . . so will your team and your organization. Those consequences include staffing crises, tension, frustration, poor patient care, absenteeism and tardiness, gossip, lack of trust, rebellion, etc. Make an intentional effort to connect with your team. It beats the alternative!

None are so old as those who have outlived enthusiasm.

—*Henry David Thoreau*

Ask an employee, "What do you like least about your job?" You may be able to make a difference.

Find a staff member's strength and let her know what an asset it is to your team!

Create a Leadership Specialist position to serve as the resource person for current and future leaders throughout the facility. This person is a consultant for leadership issues and teaches such topics as conflict resolution, building trust, mentoring, team-building, etc.

Lead with a HIRE PURPOSE: Never hire without doing thorough reference checks. Do you think references only make positive comments? You'd be surprised! The key is in asking the right questions. Target your job-related concerns. The most important question in a reference check is, "If you had a position that he was qualified for, would you hire/rehire him?" Make sure you get a signed release from the applicant *before* contacting references and ask questions related to job performance. Use professional references only. Reference checks are a useful tool to assess the quality, reliability, and long-range potential of your candidate!

Real leaders, respectfully and with the purest of motives, tell team members what they need to hear . . . what will help them grow. Most people won't do that. Someone who has only their best interests in mind will.

Ask yourself, "Why would someone want to work for me?" Work diligently to build upon that list.

Team members are responsible *to* each other, not *for* each other.

Employees like autonomy . . . don't micromanage.

Who believed in you more than you believed in yourself? Didn't you always want to do your absolute best for that person? Believe in your staff. They will go the extra mile for you!

Say, "I'm sorry." Never hesitate to apologize when it is **appropriate**.

Be crystal clear in communicating your team values and do it often.

Learning is one way to improve ourselves. Unfortunately, the need to learn doesn't get our attention the way a crisis does. But if you do it, you will be better equipped to handle a crisis. We *react* to a crisis; we must *take action* to learn.

Read *Developing the Leader Within You* by John C. Maxwell.

In conflict resolution, employees need to hear the truth. Without it, change will not occur and neither will growth. Developing people is one of the most important aspects of your role. You serve as a mirror and must objectively relate truth to your staff. It is vital to the growth of your team and to your success as a leader. Remember to target the behavior, not the person.

How do you spend your time? Spend it wisely. It's indicative of what you'll be doing in five years.

Make yourself necessary to somebody.

—*Ralph Waldo Emerson*

Admit when you are wrong. If not, your employees may get the wrong impression about you . . . that you think you are always right. They already know that is not the case!

Ask a team member, "What motivates you?"

Conflict occurs when two people try to be understood at the same time. They both want to be heard and neither wants to listen to the other side. When you listen with the goal of understanding first, you make an immediate impact on the outcome.

Leave your ego at home.

Don't be a critic; be a coach.

Stop by a bakery and take donuts to work tomorrow morning. Next month, choose a different shift and do the same! Mark your calendar. You will see many surprised faces and be the topic of conversation for quite some time!

The greatest good you can do for another is not just to share your riches, but to reveal to him his own.

—*Benjamin Disraeli*

TROUBLED is the face of a leader without purpose.

As caregivers, your staff gives all day long. In order to send them out to do a job, you must continually replenish, feed, and nurture them. A staff without nourishment will eventually have nothing left to give. Teach, give positive feedback, and show that you care.

Don't take yourself too seriously.

Perform without fail what you resolve.

—*Benjamin Franklin*

Are you losing valuable employees because you can't make the tough decision to release a problem employee? Leaders must make those calls. Always make decisions based on the good of the team. And because of a difference in values, another job with different responsibilities will be a better fit for this person.

It's a win/win situation!

The difference between what we do and what we know to do would solve most of our problems.

You can't make anyone do anything. However, you can ignite change in others by making changes in what you do. The results can be incredible!

Build trust in your team by trusting their competence and their judgment. They will try hard to meet your expectations.

It's an impossibility . . . visionaries can't be in a rut!

Real leaders think of their team members first.

Crisis is the warning siren of life that screams, "Something isn't working! It's time for a change!" Don't be satisfied to just get through the crisis. Be proactive. Assess what happened, then act to make the needed adjustments.

Don't ask an employee to do anything that you would not do. Shock your staff! Make a patient's bed or pass out meal trays today. There's no quicker way to ignite positive chatter on your unit!

Learn everything you can about your team. No two people are alike. Find what motivates and what is important to each member as a person.

He who has a why to live for can bear almost any how.
—*Friedrich Nietzsche*

Educate your staff about their responsibilities in retaining teammates. Being courteous, respectful, dependable, trustworthy, etc. all go a long way in improving a person's work environment. Immediately point out and address negative behaviors that wear down a team. An employee will leave if teammates create a hostile environment. Remind them that working with a full staff is easier on everyone. They can make a difference!

Incorporate a yearly group retention bonus for your staff. If all team members remain employed until the year's end, the entire group receives a check. You will see a difference in attitudes, support, and retention!

Read *Boundaries,* a book by Henry Cloud and John Townsend.

As for the best leaders, the people do not notice their existence. The next best, the people honor and praise. The next, the people fear, and the next the people hate. When the best leader's work is done, the people say, "We did it ourselves."

—*Lao-tzu*

Have staff members form a Rewards & Recognitions Program. They can create a list of their favorite rewards and, using the values to be modeled, determine what behaviors to reward. One catch . . . each staff member must reward another staff member at least quarterly. Watching for good results in others is a great focus and builds a strong team!

Passion is contagious . . . get some!

Don't complain to your staff about administration. They will do what they see you do. Remember that administration, your staff, and you are all a team.

Was there a person in your life who was instrumental in some of the right decisions you made? Be that person for one of your staff members.

VALUE the differences in your team members. A professional football team made up of 11 quarterbacks will not make a touchdown.

Treat your staff like volunteers. They can get another job within 24 hours.

Go to *www.baudville.com* as a resource for praise, recognition, and rewards. Give freely and often!

Listen to your words. Use "we" instead of "I" whenever possible. Show that you value and acknowledge what your team members do.

Recruitment is sales; retention is leadership. Nurses don't want *things* (perks, sign-on bonuses, etc.)—that gets them there. They want quality of work life—that keeps them there. It's up to you!

What can you do today to show your staff that they are valued, respected, and trusted?

The best gift you can give your team is your time.

Never address issues when you are angry.

Be consistent and choose to do right every time. Occasionally, the right decision is not the popular one, but stick to your principles anyway.

Showing respect encompasses many actions such as listening, taking time to understand, sharing your views with tact, and being open. As you give respect and show that you view your staff as professionals, the trust level you have with them will grow. Soon, their respect for you will grow in return.

Never hang someone out to dry to save face. It's a character issue.

Be positive. You set the tone for your unit(s).

Many leaders are thrust into their first management role with little or no preparation. You are ultimately responsible for what you know. Make it a priority to learn everything you can about being a leader. The best thing about leadership education is that you can enhance both your personal and professional life if you live what you learn!

Watch the movie *Remember the Titans.* It's a compelling lesson in leadership and teamwork.

Keep your fears to yourself, but share your courage with others.

—*Robert Louis Stevenson*

The next time you see a frown, counteract it with a smile. Then find something positive to say about that person at that very moment.

A leader is a coach. Successful coaches teach constantly . . . before, during, and after the game. Use every opportunity to teach something new and add value to a team member.

Reward staff members who mentor others. It is challenging, time-consuming, and one of the most important roles on your unit!

You won't get respect until you give respect. It's that simple.

Teamwork means working together towards a common purpose. It means you can count on each other. It means that you can share your ideas, disagree, say how you feel, and be listened to. It also means being understanding enough, focused enough, and tough enough to make a decision based on what's best for the team.

When you give advice to others, heed it. That's integrity . . .
talking the talk *and* walking the walk.

Treat others fairly.

Encourage staff to share ideas and frustrations with you.

NOTHING or nobody can help
a leader with a hardened heart,
without her permission.
Choose to build relationships
instead of barriers.

If you lead, learn something new every single day about leading.

Whatever makes us either think or feel strongly adds to our power and enlarges our field of action.

—Ralph Waldo Emerson

Share your vision with staff. Share it often. And then again!
By keeping the vision in front of your staff, you will keep them moving forward and looking ahead.

The journey to your goals changes you more than achieving your goals. It's called growth!

The investment you make in your staff will live on long after you are gone.

You simply cannot over communicate. Use several forms of communication . . . face-to-face, e-mails, memos, sticky notes, cards, bulletin boards, etc. The different generational preferences in communication will be covered!

When you praise a team member, remember to mention specifically what he did right. That way he will know exactly what behavior to repeat. For example, instead of saying, "You did great today," you might say, "I noticed how you spent extra time with Mr. Martin's family in the waiting room. I could tell that it meant a lot to them."

Are you developing a new leader? Why not step out of your leadership role for an upcoming meeting and ask her to step in? She will see that she can do it and . . . she may even like it!

A man without a purpose is like a ship without a rudder.
—*Thomas Carlyle*

Ask a staff member, "What do you like best about your job?"

Suggest that your team create a basket filled with goodies for another department in the hospital to show appreciation for them. Have every team member sign a card and add a comment. First, the staff of the other department will be shocked and amazed. It will definitely get their attention. Many will reap the rewards from this one kind act: you foster respect, add value to others, show you care, and improve work relationships. Everybody wins!

Make a decision to grow professionally. And remember, doing nothing *is* a decision . . . a decision *not* to grow.

In ten years, what will your staff remember about you?

Give credit to your team.

Bring in outside speakers to present topics for employees hospital-wide to bridge the gap between their personal lives and their work lives: financial planning, parenting teens, easy gourmet meals, computer skills, speaking, writing, etc. The employees attend during non-work hours but at no cost. The better they manage their personal lives, the smoother their work lives!

Shock your staff on a regular basis . . . be spontaneous and keep them watching to see what you will do next! The morale escalates almost immediately. Brainstorm to come up with ideas such as outrageously dressing up for a holiday and working all day in the outfit. Set a goal and if your team accomplishes it, promise to do something out of the ordinary . . . go up in a hot air balloon, do fifty laps around the hospital grounds, or buy everyone a soft drink in the cafeteria.

For an hour a week, partner an overachiever with someone you're trying to motivate. The benefits? A new relationship, exposure to new ways and attitudes, and the mentor will feel she's made a difference. Another plus . . . the mentor will be interested in her team member's success from that point on.

Lead so that years from now, a team member will look back and know that she was part of something special.

I can live for two months on a good compliment.

—*Mark Twain*

Help staff achieve their goals. Do you know what their goals are?

Leadership is caring about your staff, even when they don't deserve it.

When making decisions, don't aim for doing what's popular; aim for doing what's right.

AN ORDINARY team with a committed leader can do extraordinary things.

Lead with a HIRE PURPOSE: During the interview day, note how your candidate treats people who cannot benefit him, such as unit secretaries, people from other areas of the hospital, etc. It speaks volumes regarding his respect level for others.

Think of everyone as a customer . . . your patients, their families, physicians, your boss, volunteers, and yes, even your team. Give team members a warm welcome when they arrive, be courteous during the day, and send them home with kind words and a smile. Try it and you'll see a difference!

If you are there, be there. Give the person you are with 100% of your attention. It shows respect.

Have an open door policy. Be approachable.

Visionaries focus on benefits and the end results; they see solutions, not obstacles.

Find ways to make administration visible to your staff. Frequently invite administration to your unit's activities. Sometimes they won't be able to attend, but sometimes they will. Keep inviting! You simply must cement the fact that you are all working toward the same goal . . . quality patient care! And the more times everyone interacts, the better. Always define the purpose so that the staff and administrators have shared expectations.

Raise your own bar . . . it's a choice!

Remember when listening to two sides of a story, the truth is usually somewhere in the middle.

Retention starts during the hiring process with a good fit.
Do your homework!

You can't advance toward your purpose without being intentional and determined. If you get caught up in day-to-day activities and live in crisis intervention mode, you won't get there. You must find your way. *You must make your way!* Purpose gives meaning to what you do and serves as a compass to keep you going in the right direction. When crises, people, activities or other elements pull you from your path, it's your purpose that will guide you through the toughest storms.

If you need help, ask for it. Employees like to know
that you are human.

No employer should have better relationships with its employees
than a hospital, an organization built on the mission of respect,
care, and compassion. Work hard and live up to that reputation.

Harsh words are like weapons, only the impact and the scars are
not readily visible to the naked eye. Choose your words carefully.

Your patients know what to do . . . stop smoking, eat a low-fat diet, exercise, etc., but they don't do it. It's not that they don't want better health; they just don't want to do what it takes to achieve it. The truth is that they have two choices: (1) keep doing what they are doing and suffer the consequences or (2) change behavior, do the work, and reap the rewards of that work later.

The same principle applies to retaining staff. You've got to be disciplined and committed to do what it takes to get the results you want. Strive now to create a work environment of solid relationships, respect, trust, professional development, and encouragement. In time, your retention woes will be a distant memory!

Talents are best formed in solitude; character is best formed in the stormy billows of the world.

—*Johann von Goethe*

Give someone a smile who isn't wearing one.

Passion gives you energy that you didn't know you had. It propels you to gather information and resources; it wakes you in the middle of the night with a pouring out of ideas that you must write down at that very moment; it motivates you to grab every opportunity to move closer to fulfilling your vision.

A leader's path crosses with many but for only a short time. Use that time carefully to instill the tools they need for life . . . responsibility, honesty, trust, developing character, integrity, getting along and caring about people, continuous learning, and a positive attitude.

When you see outbursts of emotion, gossiping, and poor morale in your staff, these are symptoms. Look deeper than those symptoms and get to the heart of the matter so you can positively impact and help them deal with the real issues.

Change orders handed down are never easy to swallow. Staff members may feel hurt because the decision didn't involve them directly. That's why it is important to get staff involved as soon after the announcement as possible and keep them updated accordingly. Of course, the best case scenario is to have their input going into making such a decision.

An effective leader is a person of character, integrity, and action, adding value to the lives of others. If you add value to your staff, cause them to think, and help them grow to a higher level, you accomplish what leaders strive to achieve . . . significance!

Retention is leadership . . . it's a principle that is ongoing . . . similar to gravity. If you hold a ball up in the air and drop it, it will fall to the ground. Gravity is always working, no matter what. It doesn't matter whether you believe it is or not. Even if you don't know about gravity . . . it's very real and so are the consequences.

The same is true with leading people. If nurses are getting a fair wage, but aren't in a nurturing, growth-oriented environment where they feel valued and respected, and part of a team, they will leave. Ask yourself, "Do local nurses drive long distances to work elsewhere?" If so, the reality is—it's time to make significant changes in your leadership. You may not believe it . . . or at the very least even consider it. But if you start building staff relationships today, you can reap the rewards of your investment in the very near future.

Read *Who Moved My Cheese* by Spencer Johnson, M.D. and Kenneth H. Blanchard.

Practice AAA Leadership: Autonomy, authority, and accountability go hand in hand.

Lead with a HIRE PURPOSE: When interviewing potential employees, don't make promises you can't keep. Make sure you can meet the expectations on the back end that you have sold them on the front end. If you can't, they will quit. Develop ways to assess that what you're selling is, in fact, a reality.

Change ignites fear in the most confident and positive among us.

He has a right to criticize who has a heart to help.

—*Abraham Lincoln*

If you spend all of your time putting out fires and meeting deadlines, building relationships with people is a distraction. Find time for your staff each day, no matter how many meetings you have.

Venting is crucial for a successful change process. Listen, listen, and listen again. Staff must feel understood. This defusing agent is your biggest asset during change. Their fears will come out loud and clear. Many times the fear is much bigger than what could actually happen. Other times they are right on target. Either way, you need to know what their concerns are so that you can address them and help them through it.

Change is a learning experience . . . a growing process. You'll see a side of people you didn't know existed. Keep in mind that it's in the difficult times that true character is revealed. And yes, negativity is challenging; fear is powerful. But if you encourage, listen, show you care, maintain open lines of communication, and keep the vision in front of them, you and your staff will emerge stronger and on a more positive course!

Building strong relationships requires speaking truth, even when you don't want to. Address issues, resolve conflict, and break down barriers.

Lead on purpose!

Great teams are disciplined. They train, continuously learn new and better ways to do things, pay the price at practice, work on weaknesses, and improve their strengths. When game day comes, that preparation pays huge rewards. What steps can you take to prepare your team for the challenges they will face?

Vision is all about growth—and stretching. As long as you have a vision you won't be stagnant. Never keep things status quo. It's a fact: you cannot grow if you remain in your comfort zone. And when you tread in the area of achieving a vision, you are anything but comfortable. That's what makes it scary and exciting at the same time. It pushes you and your team to another level. You grow by going into uncharted territory and accomplishing that vision . . . and by making mistakes along the way. And that's okay.

If you're a Chief Nursing Officer, each week have your managers find a staff member doing something positive and notify you. Then personally send a letter or, better yet, go in person to that employee and communicate, "Erika told me how you spent extra time with your OB patient. I understand that she really connected with you. I know it was important to have you there, especially when she couldn't take her baby home right away. I appreciate your caring attitude!"

THE HUMAN SPIRIT, consistently nurtured and developed, is a source of inspiration, encouragement, self-control, patience, loyalty, gentleness, kindness, and a genuine concern for people.